stars at last

jessica jocelyn

Stars At Last
Copyright © 2024 Jessica Jocelyn
All rights reserved. No part of this book may be reproduced or used in any matter without the written consent of the copyright owner.
ISBN: 979-8-9879305-8-8

Cover design: Jennae Cecelia
Edited by: Shelby Leigh
Fonts by: saltandpepperfonts

for the daughters who raised themselves

part 1 mothering me   1

part 2 mothering you   81

Foreword

Beyond biological connection, a mother is a caregiver, nurturer, and protector, playing a central role in a child's development. When a mother is unable or unwilling to provide the emotional, physical, or developmental support a child needs, it leaves a deep pain—an invisible wound that lingers in the mind and soul, following them throughout life. This wound creates a desperate longing for a love that only a mother can provide.

As someone who has spent her life aching from the wound her mother created, it is a profound honor and privilege to be part of this powerful and ultimately hopeful collection by Jessica Jocelyn. She guides readers through the agony and confusion of being rejected by one's own mother, while revealing the love and purpose found in choosing to be different for one's own daughter—a journey that is both heartbreaking and profoundly healing.

Behind the beautiful words in this collection is an even more beautiful woman—a mother who has turned back time. Through the innocence of her daughter's eyes, she chooses to end the cycle, by giving her daughter the love and care she never received.

An unmothered little girl, whose sky was always black, now holds the hand of her own little girl, and together, they see the stars at last.

xo

Rose Brik
author of "*My Father's Eyes, My Mother's Rage*"

part 1:
mothering me

stars at last

there is a house with walls made of glass
and floors made of eggshells.

and inside that house lives a mother
who loves on her own terms.

the children in the house are tied to her
with a string that only they can see.

they are made from her flesh
and born carrying her pain.

love is having a daughter
and I was my mother's possession.

my first memory was of her face
contorting under all her tears.
her breath hot on my neck,
her anguish swallowing us both.

she looked into my eyes
and I let out a nervous smile.
her tears stopped and she moved on with
her day.

from then on, I was the rock.
a rough selenite absorbing her pain,
a tiny therapist,
a pill to make it all go away.

my first steps were on a tightrope,
balancing over the circus I was born into.

each step calculated
so I wouldn't be distracted
by the chaos down below.

one foot forward, arms stretched wide,
just trying to make it to the other side.

a fine performance, indeed.
the first of many.

entertainer by nature,
masquerader by blood.

I am convinced
that I was born from love.
I saw it once,
pictures in a secret pink photo album.

I saw the love,
the way they looked at each other.
it had to have been real at one time.

somewhere between me being created
and me being born, there was a shift
and my parents each wanted different things:
she wanted everything he promised her
and he wanted anything but.

somewhere in the middle of all that,
there I was
entering a world of broken promises
that fed my soul with disappointment.

mama said I had the curse.
the one where I screamed uncontrollably
throughout the night as a baby.

she couldn't handle the screams
so I was taught to keep them inside.

the curse never lifted.
I felt everything too deeply,
and tears flowed too often.

smells burned my nose
and made my stomach turn.

loud noises rattled my bones so violently
that I wished I could reach inside of me
and hold them still.

seeing roadkill
made me want to lie down
and die next to them.

it was definitely a curse,
how painful everything felt
to my small heart.

I'm sorry, mom, I forgot you are the victim.
you are the only one in this family who hurts.
you are the only one who bleeds.

I'm sorry, mom, I forgot you are the victim.
you are the one who felt the most pain
when he left us.
it was hardest on you
because you had to listen to us cry.

I'm sorry, mom, I forgot you are the victim.
how silly of me to come to you
when my heart was broken.
how naïve of me
to believe you might help me feel better.

I know you're too busy
with a broken heart of your own.

the more my mother pushed me away,
the harder I'd try to earn her love.

she'd recoil from my touch
and turn away from my tears.

I was so convinced that if she knew
how much I needed her love,
then maybe she'd finally give it to me.

brick by brick,
my parents built the house we lived in.
but
the same hands my parents used
to build our home
are the same ones they used to destroy it.

they say children are born
with innocence.

but innocence is lost
while bearing the burdens
that were never supposed to be yours.

my mother didn't hit me,
but she made everything about her.

my mother didn't hit me,
but she told me my memories weren't real.

my mother didn't hit me,
but I could feel her anger
before she even opened her mouth.

my mother didn't hit me,
but she told me I was a failure
just so she could feel better about herself.

my mother didn't hit me,
but her silence for days
was louder than her yelling.

my mother didn't hit me,
but her jealousy is a unique pain
I'll never be able to process.

in nature, some mothers eat their young.
my mother preferred to keep her prey around.

she needed soldiers to fight
all the wars inside her head.

are you a daddy's or a mama's girl?

neither. I'm a grandma's girl.

she'd kiss my hands and hold them to her chest as she prayed for me. she'd cook me warm meals to feed my body and write me poems to feed my soul.

but most importantly,
I never once had to question if she loved me.

she always made sure I knew.

two sisters were sitting in the grass.

"do you think we're together in every universe?"
one quietly asked the other.

after thinking for a bit, the other sister said:

*"if we come back as flowers,
we will grow in the same garden
and laugh when butterflies tickle us.*

*if we come back as nature,
I will be the clouds in your storm.*

*and if we come back as fruit,
we will grow on the same vine.*

it could never be possible that we aren't together."

stars at last

I'm older now,
the oldest daughter
ready to pounce.
I'm always nearby
always listening.
waiting
waiting
waiting
for the fight to escalate,
for the right time to step in.
waiting
waiting
waiting
crash
there it is.
I run in and I unleash words
hoping they penetrate like arrows.
I'm only met with laughter;
come on, try me, you're weak
just like your mother.
my heart pounds in my throat
as I tell him truths he can't swallow
and it ends how it always does:
me absorbing the force of his hands
so my mother never does.

I sat on the floor of my room
in an endless loop,
begging god to come save me.
sometimes I'd have the courage
to tell an adult.
they told me to pray more.
so I did.
I prayed.
I sat.
I was hit.
I cried.
I prayed.
I sat.
I was hit.
I cried.
I prayed.
I sat.
I was hit.
I cried.
I prayed.
I sat.
I was hit.
I cried.

I hoped one day someone would save me.

as a child,
I received looks of disgust from my parents.
stop being so weird!
what's wrong with you?

when I almost felt safe
with other kids on the playground,
there were the words again:
stop being so weird!
what's wrong with you?

a mask soon became my shield;
who I was depended on where I was
or who I was with.

I studied every situation,
analyzing it in seconds,
and quickly assimilated to it.

when I would come home,
I didn't realize that the crippling exhaustion
was from me taking the mask off.

my parents would just call me lazy,
but they didn't have any idea
the amount of work I was putting in
just to exist.

my brain is a roller coaster
stuck on repeat.

the thoughts are on an endless loop
bouncing back and forth
creating a torture chamber in my head.

I fear the thoughts will escape
through my mouth
or worse
through my hands.

these obsessions and compulsions
are a roller coaster I want to jump from,
but I'm strapped in permanently.

in between storms,
my mother comes back to me.

we laugh and we play
and I can almost swear she loves me.

I grasp on to every second I can
until I see the next storm on the horizon
coming to take her away.

my mother scares me when she's angry.

when she screams
"look what you're making me do!"
while speeding in the car.

when she tells her new husband what I did
so he can correct me with his hands again.

when she laughs every time I threaten
to call the cops.

my mother scares me when she's angry
and she's angry all the time.

mom,
tell me how to live in this world.
tell me how to just be
because it hurts to exist.

hold me;
squeeze me tight.
bring me to your chest
and tell me it will be okay.
that you'll always be here to teach me the way.

hold my hand and help me walk;
please don't leave me behind.
tell me what to do when my heart gets broken.
remind me that the sun always rises again
in the morning.

please reassure me I won't feel this way forever
please stop staring at me
while these tears flood into my hands,
staring at me like I've done something wrong.

my parents made mistakes
and their price to pay was me:

a girl crippled by anxiety
from constantly walking on eggshells,
wondering what to say next
so no one gets upset.

a girl exhausted by fight or flight
wondering if today's the day
that validation will come
without the use of a pill.

you say I'm so mature for my age
like it's a compliment
but you don't know the speed at which
my childhood passed me by
and pushed me to be older than I am.

mom, there are monsters in my closet
and now they're under my bed.

they got lonely
so we became friends
and now they live in my head.

they tell me to do bad things
and tell me how horrible I am.
mom, I don't think they are my friends anymore
but I don't know how to make them leave.

they say these are the best years of your life

but I can't get dressed for school without looking at myself in the mirror and wondering what boys will think or what other girls will say.

I'm so sure all the whispers are about me and can't convince myself otherwise
(they don't even know I exist).

these are the best years of your life

I whisper as my arms stick to the sleeves of my shirt while I apply mascara.

I don't know why I can't just *be,*
why my brain thinks that silence
is an invitation to relive all the trauma.

why must it whisper,
hey, remember when?
and start the rumination all over again.

I don't know why my brain
won't let me rest even while sleeping
and my dreams are interrupted
by my own screams.

how a sight, smell, or even sound
will cause my mind to relive it all,
knowing I must accept memories
that will never change.

my mother's rage bounced off the walls
in our house
and hid in all the dark corners.

it would fester in the walls
and start to eat them like mold.

she was always angry
but there was never a fire in her eyes,
only a dark, cold, emptiness
that told me
we were both scared little girls.

I wish I could wake up
and not be someone who cries
when there are empty tents at an art fair.

to not feel bad for my socks
if I lose one and they are no longer a pair.

when I accidentally step on an ant
and worry that his family will always wonder
what happened to him.

I would like to wake up
and not feel things so intensely.

sometimes I wish I could just feel nothing.

sticks and stones may break my bones
but words will make me spiral.

they spin in circles in my mind
until I am convinced they are true.

they keep me up at night and haunt my dreams
to make sure they aren't forgotten.

my depression wasn't scary when I was crying
into the night.
it became scary when the tears stopped flowing,
turning into fake smiles and attempts
to light up every room.

it became scary when I started giving away
things that meant something to me and leaving
letters where people might find them someday.

it became scary when what I felt wasn't sadness
anymore, but just a dark void,
nothing to see or feel.

the dark void brought with it impending peace
and excitement.

excitement for the relief from the exhaustion.

my depression became scary when I gave in.

I am my mother's burden.

her greatest inconvenience,
her biggest embarrassment.

instead of holding me after I swallowed all those pills, she wailed,
"why are you doing this to me?!"

she thinks I'm lazy, but it's just exhaustion.
I'm so tired from her telling me everything I do is wrong and nothing I do is right.

I am now her biggest regret,
a horrible memory she waves away when anyone speaks my name.

the oldest daughter urge to become mothers to children who never knew my womb / to grow up too fast and leave home as quickly as possible / to swallow all my pain and only release it in the dark / to be both my mother's hopes and dreams and her biggest disappointment / to be my father's collateral damage / to never forgive myself for accepting behavior I didn't deserve.

I beg my mother to fix us
but I don't think she wants to mend our bond.

I lie in my bed at night
and tears pool in my ears.

I pray to be good enough so she loves me.

if my own mother can't love me,
then what hope do I have?

this mind is chaotic, but I've learned to feel comfort during storms.

I want to be loved, but I can't stop lighting people on fire to stay warm.

I am either flying high with euphoria or drowning in unmeasurable sadness.

I want to go so far in life, but I can't stand to live another day.

I don't think I can handle another bad relationship, but I am addicted to the burn of a broken heart.

my heart is so unbalanced and getting so heavy to carry.

I'm so tired.

I ride on the back of the monster
I inherited from my mother.

I hold on tight, knowing the ride is
about to get bumpy.

he tells me there's no time for sleep,
that it's more fun to welcome the sun each
morning,
so we do.

we fly high in the sky.
there's nothing we can't do.
until it's over and we come crashing down.
we lie on the ground in silence.

"please check to see if you're still breathing,"
he whispers.

I don't.
I don't even care.

my mother wove charm into whatever
she said to the outside world.

she knew everyone was watching
and took all of her performances seriously.
she was perfection personified down to the
earrings that matched her outfits.

she worked every room effortlessly
and my friends would tell me how lucky
I was that she was my mother.

she knew how to make everyone feel
like they were the only person
in the room.

everyone except her children.

who were you before you were my mother?
who were you before all of this,
before the hate took all it could?

before your bones were picked clean
by scavenging men,
before their words and actions
hardened your heart?

who were you before the world
you worked so hard to build
broke you?

feminine rage sounds enchanting until you've seen it firsthand. my mom and I were sitting next to each other in the first row of the church at her sister's funeral. the pallbearers came over and lifted her sister's casket off the stand.

there was a scream.
it was full of anguish, regret, and deep sorrow.
a mournful sound that could only come from a woman.
it was coming from my mother.

it filled the church; it shook my bones.
her back slid down the pew and I grabbed her.
I was deafened by her screams
and scared by her rage.

her sister was being carried out of the church, but it was so much more than that. it was years and years of pain and abuse coming to a head in her life. it was her brain rewiring and taking on a different shape. she had always been a hurricane of a person but now she moved up to category five.

her feminine rage was catastrophic.
there was no beauty or justice in it.
only destruction for the rest of her life,
consuming everything in her path.

I have so much anger.

anger for my father
for mutilating my mother,

and anger for my mother
for letting those wounds
bleed on to her children.

my mother
was judge, jury, and executioner.

once you were sentenced,
you were rotten flesh
decaying under six feet of dirt.

no one could hear you,
no one could smell you,
no one could even say your name.

to acknowledge your existence
would mean you were against her.

and if you went against her,
she could make you disappear.

they say you understand life more
when you get older,
but did I just never learn
or did I just never grow up?

maybe I never grew up because I'm still stuck in the past.

everyone else has moved forward,
while deep down I'm still begging to go back.

I took pieces of everyone and everything in my life and held on even when the weight caused me to drown.

I could've swam to the surface, but preferred to sink with the comforting sadness I became addicted to.

people say, *"mental health matters!"*
but become mute to my face
and whisper behind my back
when they see my scars.

people say, *"call me anytime!"*
but who is actually awake
at two in the morning
when I'm lying on the floor crying?

they call me tough
and tell me I should be proud
of my survival.

I'm not all too sure
"surviving" is what I did.

it's a strange thing indeed
to carry a fury that isn't mine,

given to me by two people
very different from one another—
one made of oil,
one made of water.

it's a strange thing indeed
to never have experienced a touch
that told me
I was loved.

the price I paid to enter womanhood
was my soul
and my prize at the end
was rage.

they tell me I'm so brave,
but the truth is
I wish I didn't have to be.

I wish I could've just been a child.

I think my mother
thought I was supposed to fix her like a surgeon.
she gave me the job title at birth,
and abandoned me when I couldn't do it.
I was so busy drying her tears,
I didn't notice she never paid attention to mine.

I grew tired of trying
and when I threw up my hands in resignation,
she took it as betrayal
and from then on to her,
I didn't exist.

my mother looked at me
and only saw opportunity.

she placed all her regrets on my shoulders and made me carry all her shame.

there was violence in her love and it was easier to blame me for all that was wrong in her world.

when I didn't want to carry her regrets anymore and would lie on the floor crying from exhaustion, she'd point and yell:

"see! I told you she was crazy!"

I may have forgiven her for being my mother, but she has never forgiven me for being her daughter.

I wonder who I could've been had my mother loved me, had I not become the villain in her eyes.

what could I have been like had I not carried her idea that I was hard to love?

holding her trauma for her didn't make me stronger; it made me search for others who had baggage to unload as well.

it left me open to accept scraps of affection because they were all I felt I deserved.

my sisters and I were pawns in my mother's game and she'd move us how she saw fit.

leaving her also meant leaving them and if she hated me, then they needed to hate me, too.

she can erase me from their minds, but I'll never forget the day they were born or all the things I taught them. (I hope they don't either.)

I hope that one day when they grow up,
they come find me

and we get to be sisters again.

I didn't leave my childhood home all at once.

it happened slowly, in the nights when I would cry myself to sleep, begging god to take me someplace else.

little by little, it happened as I would never be alone, but still felt the deep sadness of loneliness.

it happened more as words and hands collided with my face. the need for control became greater and privacy became a four-letter word.

it happened more when my diary became public discussion.

maybe I walked away slowly because deep down I wanted them to beg me to come back. to take me in their arms, admit they were wrong and promise to change.

I was not a baby bird leaving the nest; I was a shell of a human being escaping the pain.

I lived in a time capsule.
my mother's very own
personal snow globe.

just as the pieces of the past
seemed to settle,
a trigger would give it a good shake
and all over again
we would relive the pain and the trauma.

but what could we do?
break the glass?
drain the water?

if I stayed, it would've killed me.
but, it felt like death all the same
when I had to leave her behind.

every year on my birthday,
I wonder if you remember.
I wonder if I cross your mind.

I wonder if you want to reach out,
I wonder if you think of me and smile
or if it makes the bile rise in your stomach.

I can't help but wonder these things,
though deep down I know
I probably don't cross your mind.

that's the most hurtful thought of all.

cutting you off was like
cutting off my arm.

it hurt to watch you fall from the pedestal
that you'd been on for years.

the "I need my mom" moments would arrive,
and all over again I would mourn you twice.
once for grieving who you were
and again for who you were
never going to be for me.

when I left, we broke like glass:
shards everywhere,
hands bloodied after I tried
to pick up the pieces.

I didn't know who I was
or where I would go,
but I knew I would get
to where I needed to be.

there was a part of me that missed my mother
and her laughter.

I don't think she liked me,
but she was all I had.

"you'll never make it without me,"
she hissed,
hating me for having the courage to walk away.

stars at last

I grieve for people who are still alive.

walking, talking, breathing people.
people who have cut me deep,
people who have hurt me on purpose.

I am homesick for a place
I can never go back to
and longing for a family
that can never be mine again.

I could sit here and tell you
that I was never the same
after I left the house I grew up in.

but I can't remember being
any different from this.

I always carried bags and bags
of the generations before me.

inside I am still that little girl
watching the walls cave in
screaming for someone to save her.

the greatest tragedy of my life
will be that even though
my parents will never be who I need them to be,
I will never stop wanting them.

even though they didn't protect me
and shattered my foundation,
I will never stop looking for them
in the people that I meet.

you were once the daughter
but now the daughter is me.

you were once the victim,
but now so am I.

we are now bonded by the same pain:
your mother did not love you
and neither does mine.

I want to believe there is good in my mother
and there is still love in her heart
for her children.

but not all mothers are good
and not all mothers love their children.

some view them as burdens
and place all the guilt and shame on them
just so they can sleep at night.

they don't give birth to babies;
they give birth to sacrificial lambs
and place them on platters
to feed to their demons.

I've been nose to nose with the devil,
grabbed him by the horns
and taken him down in one pull.

I've danced with the demons he sent my way
and laughed as I pushed them into fire.

but invite my mother over to play
and I will crumble to the floor.

I become the lonely child on the playground
who hangs around the bully,
because good or bad, it's still attention.

I am scared
that my mother will come out
through my mouth
and my father will come out
through my fists.

I unknowingly repeat what I haven't healed. I find comfort in the familiarity of being told I am nothing, no good, selfish. I tangle my legs in the bed sheets that belong to men who leave when they find someone easier to deal with. I sabotage hearts that are pure because I find them boring. sometimes I strike back, but if I stay, that means I prove I'm loyal. I ride shotgun on the journey even when the wheels have fallen off and my skin is bloody from the road rash.

stars at last

I was so thirsty,
so starved for love and attention
and touch.

I would seek these things in others
even when I knew it would end badly.

I was addicted to the chaos,
the back and forth,
the lows just to get to the highs.

I could only be handled in bits and pieces
and then they'd toss me aside.

that was so much better than letting them realize
I am no one they want
to be sticking around.

stars at last

my body is a graveyard
and sometimes old lovers like to visit.

they like to pick at the bones
scavenging just to make sure
nothing was left behind.

they take with them what they can find,
but leave behind the memories.

are there people out there
who fall in love slowly?

a soft, gentle burn,
a friendship blossoming constantly.

I want to know what that's like,
but I can't help but throw myself
at their feet and beg them not to leave
(when I know they will anyway)

I can't help but put my whole heart
in their hands
only for them to drop it
and tell me which body part
they'd rather hold instead.

love me, love me, love me.
I promise to love you back.

my words never come out right,
so I learned to speak with my body.
they'd tell me,
"you're so pretty, but damn you're weird."

"shhhh," I'd tell them
as I put my lips to theirs
just long enough to forget
that we needed to fill the silence with words.

when the time would come
that words were necessary,
I knew it was time to leave.
I couldn't think of anything more terrifying
than someone seeing
who I was inside.

so it was easier to just stay quiet.

my mother's blood runs through my veins.
it boils from the rage
and burns from the sadness.

it carries the gene that accepts abandonment
and teaches me to lick the wounds
of the men who cannot love me right.

I've been passed down the curse
of mending every broken person I find.
putting popsicle sticks on their broken wings
only to watch them
fly far away from me.

I want to crawl inside your skin,
rearrange your bones
and carve my name into them.

I want the pain to be so distinct
that the only way to describe it
is to call it by my name.

I feel empty.
empty of thoughts, hopes, dreams.

when your fingers slide through mine,
I can feel that
you're full of all those things.

can your thoughts please be mine?
can they fill the dark spaces in my head?
can I borrow your hopes and dreams?
can they be mine, too?

let's wake up tomorrow
and fill our time with those thoughts.
and when you take my face into your hands,
you'll say:

*"my god, you are so beautiful.
how are you so perfect for me?"*

I can never let you realize
that all the things you love about me
are all the things you love about yourself.

I've learned to be a mirror,
a piece of glass that you love to stare into.

I'm in the deep end
of your broken soul
and
I hate you
for telling me I'm beautiful
as I rip you to shreds.

stars at last

I swore I'd be different than her.

I wouldn't place my heart in the hands of men whose only consistency was being inconsistent.

I promised I'd love myself enough
to walk away the first time.

but here I am.

a magician at covering bruises with concealer,
eating lies like delicacies.

the apple didn't fall far from the tree.

stars at last

I look
and there you are in the mirror, mother,
laughing and taunting.

reminding me that even though I left,
I can never escape you.

you wove the anger
into the marrow of my bones,
biological reminders
that no matter how much I fought it,
I was always destined to become you.

if you ask me about my mom,
I will just shrug and say we don't talk.

but if you look into my eyes,

they will tell you that I never outgrew the little girl who always wanted her mother. when my heart broke for the first time, when I had a positive pregnancy test, when I hemorrhaged afterwards.

I always wanted her.

I wanted her hand to be there on my arm, to tell me she knew what it felt like and that I would make it to better days.

I could never outrun the little girl who cried out for her until my lungs collapsed, until my knees bled from being on the ground for so long.

they will tell you that inside,
I will never stop being the little girl who reaches out for her.

what do you see when you look at me?
do you see my mother?

do you see her smile?
her nose?
her contagious laugh?

or do you see

the ability to cut people with words?
the inherited mental illness?
the unrequited love as self harm?
the shame that eats the soul?

is that what you see?
because that is all I hear when you tell me
"you resemble your mother."

do you also see that I just want to be happy
but I can't?

after all, she is my mother and sadness runs through our veins.

when I met him and fell into his arms,
I could've slept for a thousand years.

I was safe.

I didn't know how to trust there was no
reason to run and the chaos was over.

my skin would itch,
not knowing how to accept his gentle flame
when I was used to snuffing them out.

I didn't understand how someone could love me.

I didn't know how to accept more
when I fully believed I deserved less.

he picked my broken heart off the floor,
handed me half, kept the other and said:

"you won't ever have to carry this
all alone anymore.
I will always carry half the weight with me.
and when you get tired and can't carry
your half any longer,
hand it to me.
I will carry it for you."

tell me where you got your scars.
no, not the ones that I can see.
tell me about the ones on your soul,
the ones you got in childhood,
the ones that shaped who you are.

tell me about the love you lost,
the one who still creeps in your dreams.
tell me your greatest fears
and where they come from.

let's get this out of the way
and lay all the ugly out for each other to see.
let our demons fall in love
and dance cheek to cheek
to the very music that haunts them.

stars at last

part 2:
mothering you

stars at last

stars at last

when I was little, I'd go outside at night and try to find the stars,
but each night was darker than the last.

I'd wish to be able to fly far from my home,
to be loved, to matter.

I never found any stars and my wishes never came true.
I eventually stopped searching.

many years later, I rode next to my newborn daughter as we headed home from the hospital.

the sky was new and
I allowed myself to search for stars once more.

when I glanced over at my daughter's face, she was already looking at me, and in her eyes, I could see the night sky's reflection.

that's when I finally saw them.

stars at last.

love is having a daughter
and she is my world.
my first memory of her
was her warmth on my skin.
she stared in my eyes,
pleading not for perfection,
but for effort.
little did she know
I would climb any mountain
just to get to her if she needed me.

my mother placed her pain in my palm and clasped her hands around mine.

"this was given to me by my mother. it was a gift and now I'm giving it to you. to be a woman is to inherit pain."

I carried that pain with me for many years. one day, I was rocking my brand-new baby daughter to sleep. her face on my chest, being soothed by the sound of my heartbeat.

I took the pain from my pocket and swallowed it whole. I could feel it burning my stomach.

I will gladly feel the pain for the rest of my life if it means I can't ever give it to my daughter.

I will never know what it is like to have my mother protect me.

but my daughter will.

motherhood ripped open the scars
of my childhood.

I had to deal with demons I didn't know were even there.

how could my father leave my mother with poverty?
why weren't we worth coming back for?
how could my mother blame us for what he did?

I am not a perfect human being
but I can't imagine hurting someone so small,
so innocent, so trusting.

I wish my parents had felt the same.

if I really am half my mother,
please let it be the good parts.

please don't let jealousy be my biggest trait
and others' happiness be my biggest trigger.

please let me see gardens in all their beauty
and not focus on just the weeds.

if I really am half my mother,
please don't let the bad parts bleed on to my daughter.

yes, you are still my mother,
and you always will be.

but, I've always been your daughter.

I can forgive that you didn't know
how to love me.
but I can't forget that you didn't even
want to learn how.

*"if you ever have a daughter,
it will be payback."*

and it absolutely is.

she is all the love I've ever tried to give
and all the love I should've received.

she is all the magic I lost along the way.

people ask
why I hurry by mirrors.
how do I explain to them
that I see you?

people say we have the same smile,
the same laugh,
the same features.
I invest thousands to change this,
though it does no good.

because no matter how fast
I run past my reflection,
there's always a split second
that I find you lurking.

if only our insides could match our outsides,
then it wouldn't be so hard
to convince myself that we aren't the same.

dear mom,

I am a mother now.

a mother to a daughter,
a little girl like I once was.

and every day she proves
I was never the problem.

may I break every family curse,
unlink every chain.
may I interrupt every cycle I inherited.
even the ones deep in my bones.

stars at last

I'll love you when it's easy,
and I'll love you when it's hard.
when I think I can't take another step,
or when I've lost my breath.

I'll love you during the good times,
when we smile and laugh.
but I'll also love you when it storms
and when you make mistakes.

I loved you when you were
only an inch long
and I am so sure
I'll love you even when
I become a distant memory.

no matter what you do,
where you go,
how old you get,
I'll love you when it's easy,
and I'll love you when it's hard.

stars at last

when you were small,
you would hug me so hard when you cried.
I'd run my fingers through your hair
and hum into your ear.

when I rocked you to sleep,
I would stroke your nose
until your eyelids grew so heavy
they couldn't stay open.

when you become a teenager,
I will hold you so hard when you cry
from your first broken heart.

I'll run my fingers through your hair,
and let you scream into the void.
I will help you power through the darkness
because I know it's the only way
to break through to the light.

mothering you
is also mothering me.
and because of you,
I have found healing
that I never thought was possible.

on our journey,
I will always let you lead the way.
I will ask if I can hug you
and let go only after you do.
I'll hold your hand
for as long as you need me to.

I don't want to be the reason
you think you must be tough,
rough, and calloused.

I want to be the one who taught you kindness
and to consider others.

that you never hesitate to
tell that woman you love her coat
or never stop being brave.

I want to be the reason
you have the skills
to loudly tell someone "no."
the reason you feel safe
because your roots run deep.

when I write poetry
about what brings light to my life,
more and more, the pages fill with your name.

thank you for coming into my life
and filling it with your beauty.

the best thing I can do for my daughter
is to love myself.

I can't hate my body
and expect her to love hers.
I can't sigh at what I see in the mirror
and think she won't do the same.

I can never let her see me place my happiness
in someone else's hands.
my peace will always come from within.

and in a world where women are torn down,
picked apart,
held to unrealistic standards,
she will be raised the opposite of how I was.

she will be complete all on her own.

my girlhood is you

to raise a daughter
is to find girlhood again.

it's putting baby curls into tiny bows,
and having tea parties with wooden cakes and treats.

it's getting mud in our toenails and making soups out of water and grass.

it's brushing her hair while telling her that she is beautiful until she looks into the mirror and smiles because she believes it.

it's collecting stickers and finding trinkets in pockets.

it's running through fields of fireflies on summer nights and whispering secrets to the moon.
it's hours of holding her when she cries from her first broken heart.

it's teaching her she is complete all by herself and anything else is just complimentary.

it's giving her the freedom to fly off into the world but also providing reassurance
that she can always return.

and there she goes,
made from my body.

running on her toes
and singing at the top of her lungs.

flowers are in her hair
as she stops to line up a group of rocks
she has found.

I feel my soul has been plagiarized
as she spins and spins.

she is still as loud as the moment I met her.
she gets to look at the world
without the lens of trauma.

she turns to smile at me and I realize
that my soulmate didn't come
in the form of a man,
but rather through her.
she has taught me
how love should feel
between a mother and her daughter.

you are my Neverland.
you are where I never grow old.
you are music and dancing
and everything fun at a party.
you are the energy that feeds my soul
and the ache in my stomach
after I've laughed so hard I can't breathe.
you are the rainbow
after the rain
and the peace I feel
just before I fall asleep.
you are the demolition I needed
to build back up and be better
and the reason
I will always get back up
and not stay down.

my biggest fear
is that one day
my daughter might write
a book like this.

stars at last

I haven't seen my mother in years
but she still haunts these halls.

she whispers in my ear
what a failure I am
and to just give it time.
the anger will one day consume me, too

I hear her laughter as she talks about a curse,
the one we are born to carry.

she says that soon, I will find the sickness
in my daughter's eyes.
one day she will hate me
and leave without a word just like I did.

may my daughter never know me
by the sound of my footsteps.

in the book of our lives,
I wish I could rewrite my siblings and me
a better beginning.

we never deserved that.
we deserved to be children.

sometimes my childhood
seems so far away
and I wonder if
it never happened.

and then I feel the tears
fall off my chin.

oh, there it is.

growing up,
when I was told I looked like my mother,
all I could hear were my father's words
telling her she wasn't good enough.
it was engrained in me
that if she wasn't good enough,
then I must not be either.

I smashed the mirror
to break the spell
and spoke to myself
with all the love in the world:

"you don't look like her.
you look like you."

I mourn the mother I will only ever meet in my dreams.

the one who wipes my tears instead of drowning me in hers.
the one who holds me in her arms instead of wasting away in mine.

she stands tall and loves me enough to fight the demons in her soul.

she doesn't ever let them win.

sometimes I wonder what I did
to deserve what they did to me.

sometimes I wonder if I really was
the bad one,
the difficult one.

sometimes I even wonder if what happened
was really all that awful.

but when I fall down that hole,
all I must do is look into my child's eyes
and ask myself if I would do to them
what was done to me.

the answer is always no.

if my mother could do her life over, she would've gone down a different path. she would've followed her heart and made different choices that she thought would bring her happiness.

if I was given the same choice,
I'd still choose you.

even on nights when I wished
to never wake up,
I'd choose you.

on the days when I was so sure the pain
of a broken heart would never end,
I'd choose you.

I'd go through every storm that ever blew my way, just because I know you'll be there on the other side. just to have the chance to grow you, to birth you, to nurture you.

in every universe, I'd choose you.

maybe nothing happens for a reason

or maybe my mother exists to remind me
who not to be for my daughter.

by not being a good mother,
she taught me how to be a great one.

this is a blood-stained
love story.
a broken fairytale.
I can't help
but still believe
that my mother will love me again.

she thinks I don't understand
but I know
that my mother is still just a daughter.

unseen and unheard by her own mother,
fighting for love and affection
and looking for them in the arms of men
who could never give it to her.

she thinks I don't get it,
but I do.
and while I understand why
she is the way she is,
I'll never accept that what should've bonded us
is what drove us apart.

and as her mind atrophied,
I watched the house of cards fall.
and as they fell, I used my body
to absorb every blow
so my daughter will never experience
the devastation of my mother's storms.

if love could've saved my mother, it never would've ended this way.

if she had fallen to her knees and said she was sorry, I would've fallen to the floor with her.

I would've grabbed her hands in mine and accepted her back into my heart.

but she rejected my hand each time I reached for her.

she let the anger and the hate eat through her body like cancer and used her last breaths to tell me she wished she had birthed something better.

the anger was all she had at the end.
it stayed by her side and carried her to peace, to a sleep she was anxiously awaiting.

it tucked her in as she let out a sigh of relief.

relief that it was finally over.

maybe in another lifetime
I am not your daughter.

maybe we pass by each other on the street
and you compliment my style
and say you wish you could be just as bold.

maybe we are just two people at the library who realize we are looking for the same book and giggle nervously as we decide who gets to leave with it.

maybe in another lifetime
I am still your daughter.

and I've turned out to be everything you ever dreamed of and you braid my hair and tie the ends off with unicorn hair ties.

maybe in another lifetime
I am the daughter that you wanted in this one.

stars at last

if heaven is real,

I imagine it's a place
where my mother can be happy.
she is a little girl with her hair
in two long braids,
bows of yellow yarn on the ends.
she laughs and is surrounded by angels
who give her endless love.
no one has hurt her;
she doesn't know the consequences
of a man's touch.
she chases the rays of sunshine
through the clouds
and never knows pain.
her brain stays perfect and innocent
and she never gets trapped inside it.
she is free.

I think that is all she ever wanted.

maybe I asked for too much
when I asked her to love me.

maybe it was too hard for her to do.

I had eyes the same color as the man
who ripped her world apart.

I represented everything she thought she'd be,
a life she was promised,
a life she was meant to have.

she couldn't handle when I grew
and when I achieved things.

loving me meant accepting her life
as it was, as it is, as it always will be.

and that was something she just could never do.

my mother said I was born too early,
but I always wondered if, deep down, she wasn't truly talking about being born before my due date.

I think she meant I arrived before she had a chance to know herself. and instead of the world at her fingertips, she now had a tiny baby.

she viewed me as a thief.

I had stolen her youth, her freedom.
I even took her name and replaced it with the word "mom."

I know she wondered who she could've been or what she could've had.

I see now that it was easier to push me away than to learn to love all the different ways her dreams were killed.

stars at last

in another universe, my mother is on the floor with me coloring in a Rainbow Brite coloring book. she is smiling and touching my cheek, her hand lingering for just a bit. she gets up to finish dinner while my baby sister sleeps in her swing. my mother puts Randy Travis on again and sings how she'll love us forever and ever. her heart is healing from my father's abandonment and she hasn't met my stepfather yet. she is present and rage hasn't claimed her.

in another universe, she is still happy.
in another universe, she stays my mother.

this isn't easy,
but I can be my own mother.
I can create security within myself
and make sure that
I'm safe and sound.

I can validate myself
and never need to seek it from others
and tell myself I'm beautiful
and powerful and strong.

the holes she forgot to fill
after she dug them,
I will fill myself.
I will be whole on my own.

we are the daughters of fathers who broke our hearts before any man could.

we are the daughters of mothers who only wanted babies—soft malleable things that could be molded and controlled.

we are the daughters who were passed down voids, but instead of leaving them empty, we planted dreams and watched them grow.

we are bones in bloom, becoming everything they said we could never be.

we are the daughters who made it.

burn the family tree down

I am the villain for not being meek
for not falling into place
with the
long line of women before me.
silence meant survival
but I don't just want to exist,
I want to live.
I am the first to start the smoke
so that my daughter
can breathe fire.

the price I paid to exist
was a mother who couldn't love me.

my karma was a daughter
made from stars.

I know you're holding on to the anger.
it came to you when you realized
you deserved more than what they gave.

it stayed because you feel it protects you.

the anger keeps people at a safe distance
so you'll never be hurt again.

when we are in survival mode,
we develop ways to get through it.

once we are out and start to heal,
we have to say goodbye
to what no longer serves us.

I hope one day you can let it go.

stars at last

I know deep down
you are waiting for that apology.

to hear the words, *I'm sorry, I was wrong.*
I know you are waiting to see those arms outstretched,
welcoming you into an embrace
that settles all the demons in your soul.

but if we need that apology to start healing,
they still have the power to dictate our lives.

especially if the apology never comes.

our closure comes from living a beautiful life in spite of the pain they have caused.

our biggest accomplishment is growing up to be nothing like them.

and maybe that is our happy ending.

stars at last

ABOUT THE AUTHOR

Jessica Jocelyn is the author of five poetry books (Chasing Wildfires, Finding Daisies, Girl (Remastered), Ever More, and Stars At Last), a proud mother, and a nemophilist. By sharing her lived experiences, she strives to deeply connect with her readers and remind them that they are not in this alone. Jessica's poetry may be hard to hear at times, but it's always healing to read. In the same vein, her past may be dark, but writing serves as her spark of sunlight. When she isn't storytelling, you can find this free-spirited goth spending quality time with her family that inspire her every day.

instagram: @letters.to.anna
tiktok: @jessica.jocelyn

other titles by the author:

the author's personal journey of the building,
destruction, and reconstruction of a family
effected by addiction told through poetry.

stars at last

jessica jocelyn

finding
daisies

decorations by
janelle parraz

poetry on healing the inner child and
breaking the cycle

jessica jocelyn

encontrando
margaritas

decoraciones de janelle parraz

the Spanish version of Finding Daisies

girl (remastered)

jessica jocelyn

poetry on childhood trauma, toxic relationships, motherhood, religious trauma, and late autism diagnosis

ever · more

POEMS ON PREGNANCY & MOTHERHOOD

jessica jocelyn

poetry on the pregnancy and
motherhood journey.

stars at last

Made in United States
Orlando, FL
16 September 2024